GW01158644

Keepsake Crafts

Buttons

KEEPSAKE CRAFTS
BUTTONS

Jo Moody

First published in Australia in 1994 by
RD Press, a registered business name of
Reader's Digest (Australia) Pty Limited
26-32 Waterloo Street, Surry Hills,
NSW 2010

© 1994 Quarto Publishing plc

A QUARTO BOOK

All rights reserved. Unauthorised
reproduction, whether in whole or in part, or
in any manner, whether mechanical, electric
or otherwise, except as permitted under the
Copyright Act or by the written permission of
the publisher, is prohibited.

The National Library of Australia
Cataloguing-in-Publication data

Moody, Jo.
  Buttons.

  ISBN 0 86438 644 3.
  ISBN 0 86438 722 9 (series).

  1. Button craft. 2. Jewelry making. I. Title.
  (Series: Keepsake crafts).

745.584

This book was designed and produced by
Quarto Publishing plc

Senior editor Sally MacEachern
Editors Geraldine Christy, Jane Royston
Senior art editor Amanda Bakhtiar
Designer Nick Clark
Photographers Paul Forrester, Chas Wilder
Illustrator Elsa Godfrey
Art director Moira Clinch
Editorial director Sophie Collins

Typeset by Poole Typesetting, Bournemouth
Manufactured in Hong Kong by Regent
Publishing Services Ltd
Printed in China by Leefung-Asco Printers
Ltd

CONTENTS

INTRODUCTION	6
MATERIALS	8
MAKING YOUR OWN BUTTONS	10
JAZZY JACKET	12
DAZZLING DJ	14
NATURAL WINNER	16
PEARLY QUEEN	18
SILVER HIGHLIGHTS	20
FANCY FOOTWORK	22
HAT TRICKS	24
BUTTONED UP	26
TASTEFULLY TRIMMED	28
ALL TIED-UP	30
ELEGANT EARRINGS	32

Hair dressing	34				
Brooch & bracelet	36	Quilted treasure	48	Boxing Clever	58
Neck & neck	38	Terrific tiebacks	50	It's a frame-up	60
Sunflower shirt	40	Hot spots	52		
Dizzy dinosaurs	42	Pretty as a picture	54		
All things nice	44	Creative cards	56		
All square	46			Button people	62
				Acknowledgments	64

INTRODUCTION

There is an amazing variety of buttons to be found in every shape, size and colour imaginable, made from many different materials including wood, horn, glass, plastic, metal and shell. They can be plain, moulded into fun shapes or carved with intricate designs, and you can even make your own.

Many people have collections of beautiful buttons, but all too often they sit unseen and unappreciated at the bottom of a box. The projects in this book will inspire you to use those buttons not merely as fastenings on clothes, but in the most innovative of ways. Antique and contemporary buttons make wonderful jewellery, for instance, and add decoration to all kinds of fashion and home accessories. The only limit to what you can do is your imagination!

SHELL BUTTONS
Shell buttons (above) have a beautiful glossy sheen. Markings can be strong and pronounced or very subtle, and the "wrong" side often looks as attractive as the right side.

NOVELTY BUTTONS
Novelty buttons (below) make ideal decoration on both children's and adults' accessories. Animals and alphabet letters used to spell out words are great fun for children's clothes.

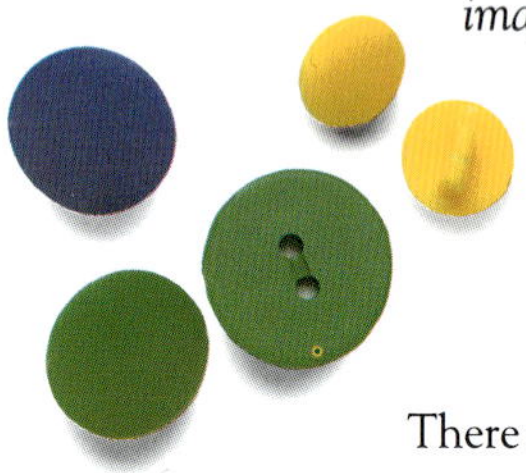

BUTTON TYPES
There are two basic types of buttons. A shank button has a loop on the wrong side, which can be moulded from the same material, as here, or made of metal. Sew-through buttons can have any number of holes, but two or four are most commonly found today.

PLASTIC BUTTONS
Plastic buttons (left and right) can be dyed to any colour, and moulded or faceted to resemble metal, glass, ivory or almost any other material. They are much lighter and less expensive than the real thing.

Introduction

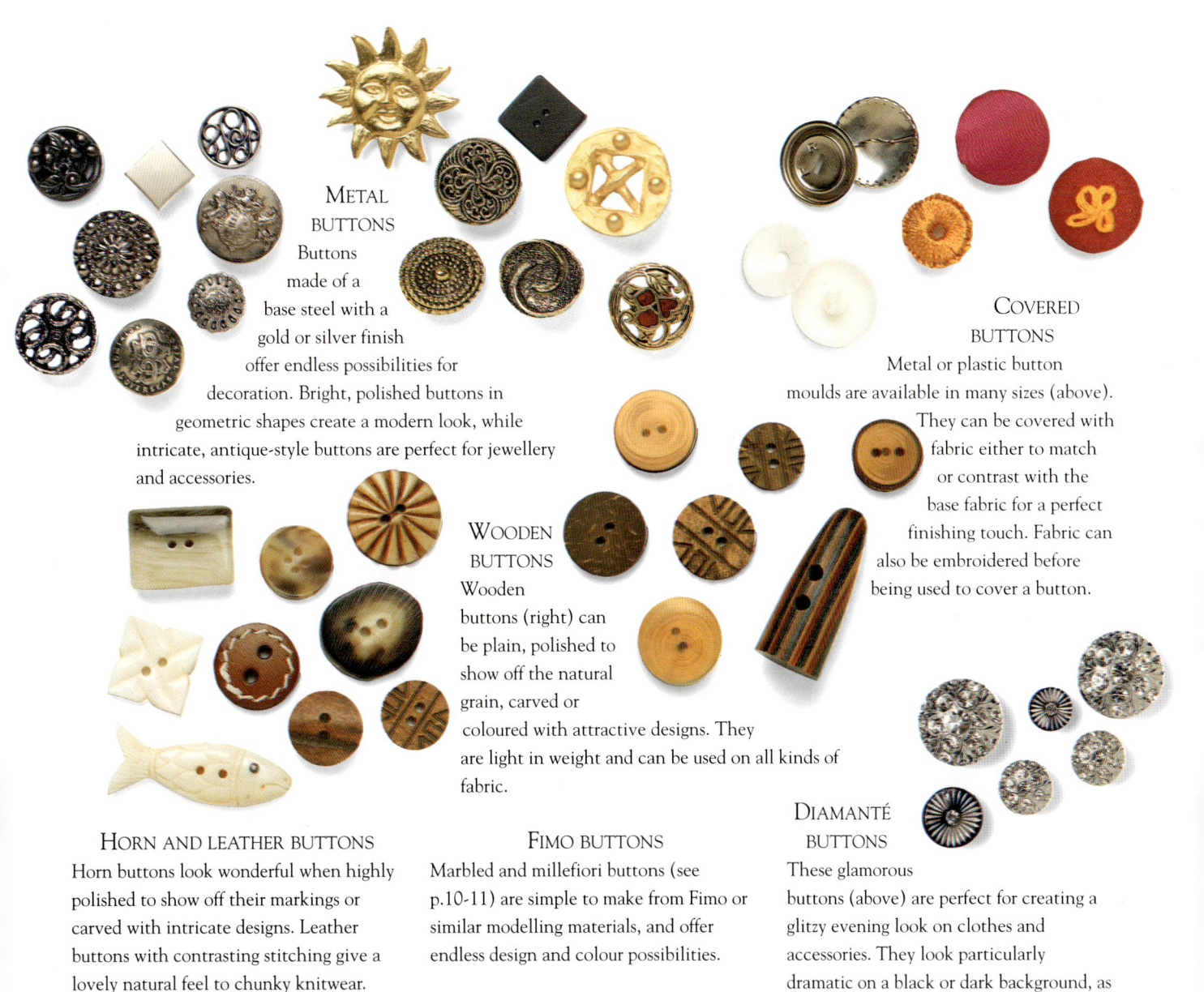

Metal buttons

Buttons made of a base steel with a gold or silver finish offer endless possibilities for decoration. Bright, polished buttons in geometric shapes create a modern look, while intricate, antique-style buttons are perfect for jewellery and accessories.

Wooden buttons

Wooden buttons (right) can be plain, polished to show off the natural grain, carved or coloured with attractive designs. They are light in weight and can be used on all kinds of fabric.

Covered buttons

Metal or plastic button moulds are available in many sizes (above). They can be covered with fabric either to match or contrast with the base fabric for a perfect finishing touch. Fabric can also be embroidered before being used to cover a button.

Horn and leather buttons

Horn buttons look wonderful when highly polished to show off their markings or carved with intricate designs. Leather buttons with contrasting stitching give a lovely natural feel to chunky knitwear.

Fimo buttons

Marbled and millefiori buttons (see p.10-11) are simple to make from Fimo or similar modelling materials, and offer endless design and colour possibilities.

Diamanté buttons

These glamorous buttons (above) are perfect for creating a glitzy evening look on clothes and accessories. They look particularly dramatic on a black or dark background, as they sparkle and catch the light.

MATERIALS

Most of the projects in this book require little in the way of specialist equipment, although there are a few items that you will find helpful. If you do not already have these in your sewing or household tool box, they are inexpensive to buy and are readily available from the local shopping centre, specialist craft outlets and by mail order.

Having the correct equipment at hand will make working the projects much easier and will also give a professional finish, so it is worth investing in the right tools before you start. Shown here are the basic items you will need.

FINDINGS

Findings are the metal components used for jewellery making, although some are decorative enough for other purposes. **1** Jump rings link various jewellery components and findings. **2** Triangle bails are used to hang thicker buttons, which will not take a jump ring. **3** Eye pins are threaded through buttons to link them together and to other findings. **4** Head pins are used in the same way as eye pins. **5** Screw clasps consist of two halves which screw together. **6** Pierced-ear wires come in various shapes. **7** Bell caps conceal multi-strand thread ends on a necklace or earrings. **8** Brooch backs provide a base for sewn or glued buttons. **9** Posts with butterfly fastenings for pierced ears. **10** Decorative clasps. **11** Screw and clip fastenings for non-pierced ears.

PLIERS

Small jeweller's pliers with fine, smooth tips are needed for working with findings, and are used to bend head and eye pins into shape, make loops, open and close jump rings and fix crimps. If these do not have a cutting edge, wire-cutters will also be needed.

BRADAWL

A bradawl is used for starting holes in leather prior to stitching on buttons.

MATERIALS

THREADS
Your choice of thread will depend on the size of buttons and the technique being worked.
1. Invisible thread is ideal for fine work, as are silk and cotton threads. **2** Nylon line has great strength and is useful for jewellery making and more unusual items such as button people (see pages 62-3). **3** Bright cotton threads can be chosen to match a colour scheme. **4** Metallic and iridescent threads add interest.

NEEDLES
The type and size of needle required will depend on the buttons (especially the size of the hole) and the materials and techniques being used.
1 Beading needles are ideal for fine fabrics. **2** Quilting needles are fine enough to go through most buttons and fabrics. **3** Leather needles, with their sharp, angled points, are useful for stitching buttons on to belts or bags. **4** Curved needles are extremely useful for decorating more unusual, ready made objects such as hair accessories and bags.

GLUES
Your choice of adhesive will depend on the materials you are using. Check the manufacturer's instructions before application.
1 Two-part epoxy glue is very strong and usually dries to a clear finish. **2** A good, general-purpose PVA-based craft glue will suffice for most projects.

SCISSORS
Good scissors are essential for working with buttons.
1 General-purpose craft scissors. **2** Small, sharp-pointed embroidery scissors are used for snipping thread ends.

MAKING YOUR OWN BUTTONS

Making your own buttons is easy and fun, and will give you the extra satisfaction of knowing that you have made a whole project yourself from start to finish. Fimo modelling clay is inexpensive and is available in a wide range of colours, making your options for button design almost limitless.

The finished buttons are baked in the oven to create a hardwearing finish that is suitable for a range of purposes, including jewellery, clothing and hair accessories. Bear in mind, however, that these buttons are hand washable and would therefore be unsuitable for an item that is likely to need frequent washing (unless you remove the buttons first).

embroider the fabric, do so at this stage so that you know where to position the stitching.

2 Run a gathering thread around the fabric edge and place the button at the centre. Draw up the thread so that the fabric is stretched tight across the button.

3 Snap the back of the mould on to the wrong side to fix the fabric securely.

COVERED BUTTONS

1 Using a pair of compasses, draw a circle of a larger circumference than the button mould, and cut it out. If you wish to

MARBLED BUTTONS

1 Knead two or three colours of Fimo modelling clay until soft and roll them into equal sausage shapes. Twist the sausages together (left). Continue to knead and twist the clay colours together until you achieve the marbled effect (right). Take care not to over-knead the clay, or the colours will blend together and you will lose the effect.

Making Your Own Buttons

Millefiori Buttons

1 To make the design shown here, take Fimo modelling clay in dark blue, green, mid-blue, red and yellow (or the colours of your choice), and then knead them until soft. Roll out thin pieces of dark blue and green clay, place them together and then roll them up to make a spiral design. stick them around the spiral as shown. Re-roll the clay gently to maintain the shape.

2 Roll out the marbled clay evenly and cut it into slices using a sharp craft knife.

3 Roll out a thin piece of dark blue clay, and roll this around the inner colours, keeping it as even as possible. Roll out the finished sausage more thinly.

3 Make holes in the buttons with cocktail sticks or wooden skewers and bake them in the oven, following the manufacturer's instructions.

If you wish, paint or spray a light, even coat of varnish over the buttons and leave them to dry thoroughly.

2 Roll out a sausage shape of red, and roll a thin layer of mid-blue evenly around it. Cut the sausage shape into several lengths. Make similar lengths of yellow clay, and, alternating this with the blue-and-red roll,

4 Cut the sausage into slices with a sharp craft knife and mould them into the button shapes of your choice. Form the holes with a cocktail stick or wooden skewer, and bake the buttons in the oven

If you wish, paint or spray the buttons with a light, even coat of varnish to complete.

JAZZY JACKET

Spice up a plain but brightly coloured jacket by adding more colour with a novel button trim. Stunning contrasts work well together, giving the jacket a totally new look.

Rows of colourful buttons on the pockets, with larger buttons on the cuffs, give this plain blue jacket a really stylish finish.

Italian designers are renowned for producing clothes with both style and humour, and it was their inspired use of buttons as decoration on clothes that influenced this jacket. You can use buttons in lots of unusual ways to add designer detail and to make a more eye-catching feature of an ordinary element. Necklines can be prettily enhanced, while hems and waistbands can be emphasized by outlining them with attractive buttons in toning or clashing colours. Collars, cuffs and pockets can be given the same treatment – cover them lavishly with buttons for a really ornate finish, or just dot the buttons about for a more understated look.

Brightly coloured buttons have been used to decorate the pocket tops and cuffs on this jacket. Using bold colour on top of another bold colour usually requires some courage, but the result can be sensational, as you can see here. The buttons look good enough to eat, like brightly coloured sweets, and add a brilliant jazzy finish. For those who prefer a less striking design, simply swapping the original buttons for more colourful ones will add some individual flair.

The buttons can have shank or hole fittings and need to be sewn in place overlapping each other to cover the area completely. If you decorate the pocket tops of a jacket, be sure to sew the buttons securely, as they will get quite a lot of wear with hands going in and out of them frequently.

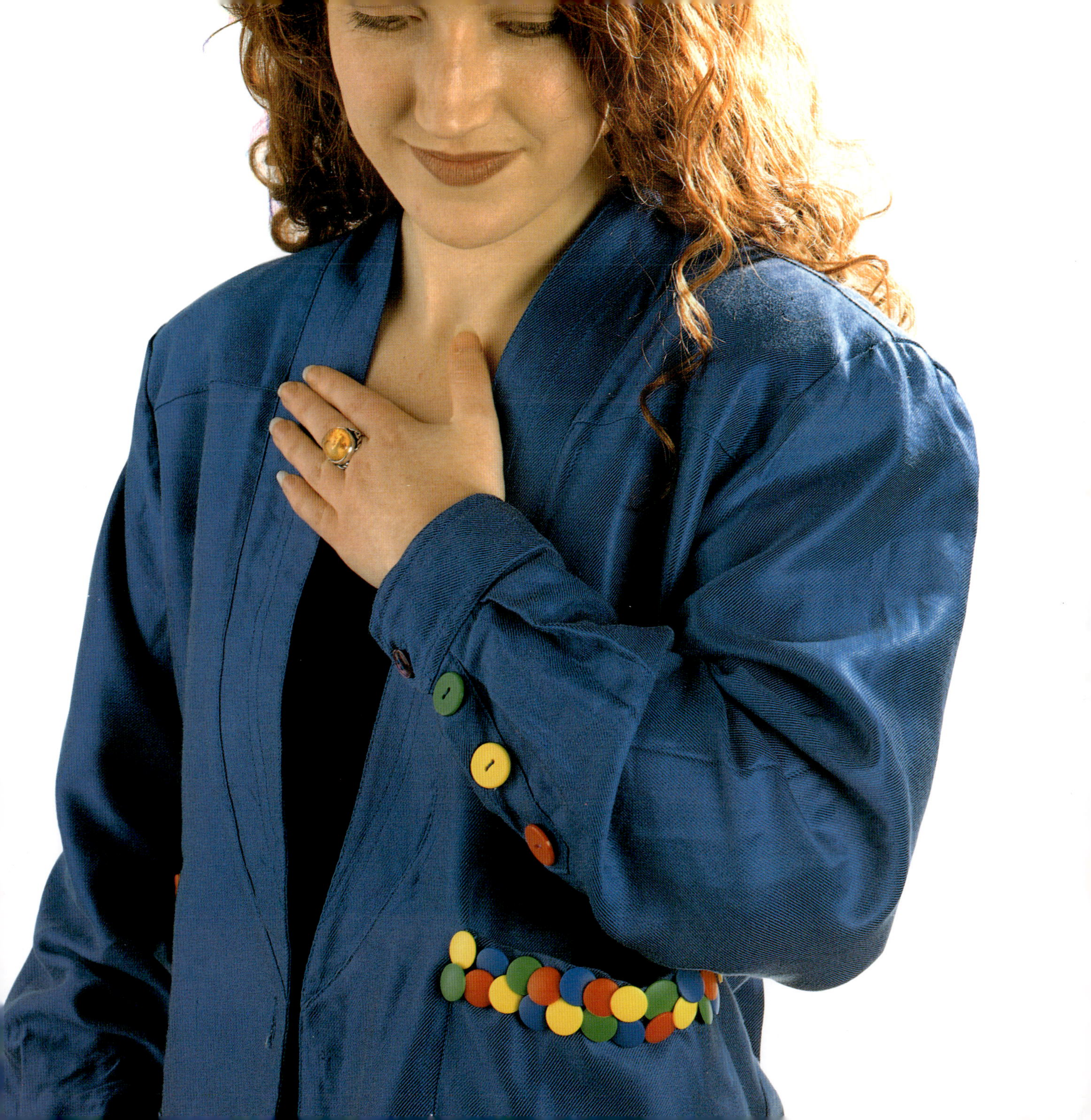

BUTTONS

An ordinary dinner jacket comes to life with the help of some strategically placed diamanté buttons. These add wonderful light-catching sparkles, and contrast beautifully with the black fabric. Other buttons could be substituted for a different look – gold or bright colours would be very effective.

Having scoured nearly-new shops, charity shops and various fairs, I discovered this classic dinner jacket with matching trousers at a car-boot sale. The suit was a real find at a bargain price. It was in good condition and, after dry-cleaning, looked brand new. Many people throw out amazingly good clothes, and it is easy to become addicted to searching out original pieces to customize by adding your own personal mark.

This jacket was given a more feminine feel by decorating the silky satin revers with an assortment of diamanté and modern clear perspex buttons to add glamour, while still retaining the sleek, stylish, tailored look. The jacket originally fastened with a traditional *passementerie* braided button which was rather the worse for wear, so this was replaced with a single spectacular diamanté button to complete the sophisticated look.

A more understated effect can be achieved by simply swapping the original fastening buttons and those on the cuffs for more elaborate or opulent ones. You could add further interest by decorating the breast pocket and perhaps the side pockets with additional buttons. The diamanté buttons used here add a touch of sparkle, but pretty mother-of-pearl buttons, with their lustrous sheen, or antique silver or gold buttons, would look just as stunning.

On this jacket, the buttons on the revers were sewn in place individually with a beading needle and a fine invisible thread of the type often used for machine embroidery. A single strand of silk embroidery thread in a matching colour could also be used. The important point is to cause as little damage as possible to the fabric, in case you decide one day to revert to the original look.

DAZZLING DJ

Glittering diamanté buttons add jazz and pizzazz to a second-hand dinner jacket, turning it into a designer-style original that is perfect for glamorous evenings out.

Natural Winner

Waistcoats are extraordinarily versatile items of clothing – they can be sharp and tailored, casual and unstructured, or dressy and elegant, and look as good worn with a business suit as they do with jeans.

A perennial fashion favourite, the waistcoat has come a long way from its traditional roots – the simple tailored version worn under a suit jacket has been banished to the city and has made way for a more colourful cousin. A waistcoat can be dressed up or down to suit the occasion and the character of its owner, turning it into an accessory rather than just an item of clothing.

Inspired by attractive but expensive designs available in the shops, this waistcoat was made up in a loose-weave raw silk from a simple dressmaking pattern. The soft beige fabric toned beautifully with a set of horn buttons that I had in my collection, but some wooden buttons and others which had a natural feel also complemented the material particularly well, so I decided to use all the buttons to create a totally original and eye-catching waistcoat with a fashionable natural theme.

In this instance, the waistcoat was already completed, so the buttons had to be added afterwards. The tricky part is sewing them to the top fabric only so that ugly stitching does not show through on the lining, which would prevent the garment from being worn open. You may find it easier to make up the waistcoat only partially, joining the lining just to the front edges before adding the button decoration.

NATURAL WINNER

A selection of wood and horn buttons emphasizes the natural feel and soft, subtle colouring of this chic waistcoat in rich raw silk.

The lining will then conceal the stitching once it is sewn into place.

Lay out the waistcoat in front of you and experiment with different designs, bearing in mind that too few buttons will not create much of an impact, while too many may distort the fabric. Sew on the buttons with a strong cotton thread.

It is safest with this type of decoration to wash the garment carefully by hand in lukewarm water and to leave it to dry flat, but remember to check first whether the buttons can be washed, or whether they should be dry-cleaned.

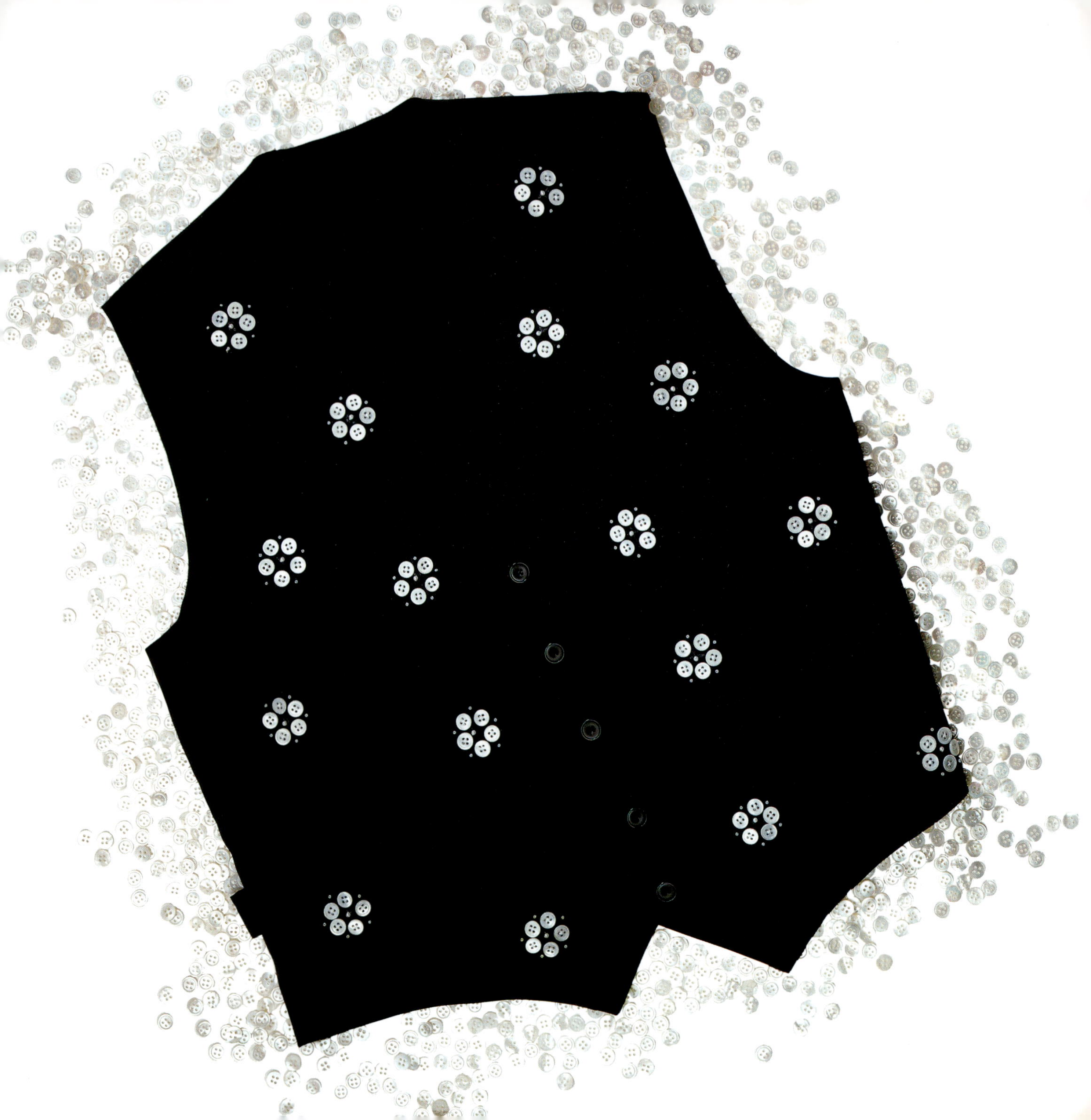

PEARLY QUEEN

A plain-coloured waistcoat can be transformed with the help of an eye-catching button design. Light, bright buttons look particularly effective on black fabric for a special occasion.

This plain black waistcoat has been decorated with small mother-of-pearl buttons clustered in stylized floral motifs, each of which is highlighted with delicate seed pearls.

Plain black fabric can be decorated in all manner of ways to create totally different looks. Mother-of-pearl buttons and seed pearls were used here, but small gold buttons and rocaille beads could also be incorporated into this or a similar design for a more ornate and dressy finish.

This simple waistcoat was made using a basic paper pattern. First cut out all the pieces from the fabric and lining material, and then lay out the two front pieces. Remembering to allow for the seams, place the buttons on the front pieces and experiment with different patterns and designs until you have decided exactly what you want. Mark the position of all the buttons with tailor's chalk, and sew them in place before joining the front pieces to the lining (in this way, the unattractive stitching on the wrong side will be concealed inside the lining). If you wish to update a waistcoat that you already have in your wardrobe, as in the previous project, be sure to make tiny, neat stitches to prevent an ugly finish that would show if the waistcoat were worn unbuttoned.

Complete the waistcoat, following the instructions on the pattern, and then wear your finished design with pride in the knowledge that it is a one-off original.

BUTTONS

Square and round buttons in varying sizes highlight the cable pattern on this handmade sweater. The tassels, which were simply made from three bead strings threaded in place under the button, add the perfect finishing touch.

SILVER HIGHLIGHTS

Give a favourite sweater a bright new look by personalizing it with decorative buttons. Choose interesting shapes and textures to add designer flair, or bright, clashing colours for a more fun look.

Buttons can be added as decoration to both bought and hand-knitted sweaters. Use the buttons as simple trims around collars, cuffs and welts, or to accentuate the texture, as in this example.

Choose colours to co-ordinate or to add richness. Wood and horn buttons go well with cream or tweedy Aran knits, for instance. The lustre of shell buttons enhances almost any garment, as do precious metals, especially those with antiqued finishes. Primary colours in bold shapes provide dramatic contrast to plain black or dark fabric such as navy or bottle green.

Lay the sweater out flat and experiment, placing buttons here and there to see how they look. Let the design and pattern on the sweater guide you, and try to highlight any interesting detail. If you are decorating a plain stocking-stitch sweater, be brave and dot buttons all over it, or create an intricate patchwork effect. Choose buttons of a suitable weight for the type of garment – big, heavy, metal buttons look best on chunky wool, while mother-of-pearl or glass buttons are ideal for finer yarns.

Once you have decided on the design, sketch it out roughly on paper and then, following this guide, sew on each button individually using a strong thread in a colour to match the garment.

The finished sweater will need to be washed with care by hand and dried flat, or dry-cleaned (refer to the recommendation on the ball band if the sweater is a hand-knit, or to the manufacturer's instructions if it is a bought item). Be sure to bear the aftercare in mind when selecting your buttons, as this will affect your choice.

Classic shoes can be cleverly updated with simple button decoration. Whether you choose antique buttons to add a classy, expensive touch, or witty buttons for sheer fun, they can transform a plain pair of shoes into something extra-special.

FANCY FOOTWORK

Two antique-style buttons sewn to the fronts of the court shoes below create an instant designer feel. Diamanté buttons could be similarly placed for elegant evening shoes.

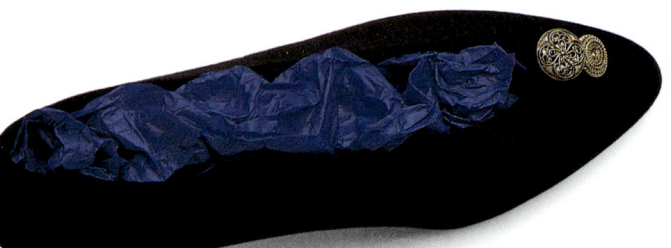

Stuck all over basic court shoes like large polka dots, the white buttons below really come into their own.

Buttons are incredibly versatile, and come in such a wonderful array of colours, shapes and sizes that they shouldn't have to be confined to functional uses on clothes. With a little ingenuity and artistic licence, you can create your own unique high-fashion footwear to step out in style.

The beauty of shoe decoration is that it does not always involve lots of buttons, nor do they need to be a matching set. One or two buttons strategically placed can make an ordinary pair of shoes look exclusive, as the shoes opposite show. These buttons had shank fittings and were sewn on using a curved needle and strong button thread.

The large white buttons on the shoes in the middle were rather uninspiring and looked ugly on a jacket, but created a chic and much-admired pair of shoes. Make sure that shoes are completely clean and free of dust before gluing on the buttons, and use a waterproof adhesive.

I snapped up the "watch" buttons shown above on sight, as I hadn't seen anything like them before. These had shank fittings, and I attached the chain to the shanks before sewing the buttons in place with the aid of pliers and jump rings (used for making jewellery – see pages 8-9). This was a perfect way in which to display an awkward number of buttons.

This type of decoration on shoes is fine for occasion wear, but will not stand up to a lot of heavy use – however, nor will some of the most expensive shoes that you can buy in the shops!

These fun, watch-design buttons, with the addition of some old necklace chain, make a pair of shoes witty and stylish.

BUTTONS

Give last season's hat a brand new look by using buttons to add style and humour. Be bold and daring or subtle and understated with your design, and create an original head-turning accessory!

HAT TRICKS

Buttons sewn to hat bands can create a range of effects. Natural-coloured buttons complement the "pot" hat above perfectly, and wood and horn buttons suit the trilby on the right.

A few buttons and a little imagination can transform a very ordinary hat into a trendsetter with designer flair. You could cover the whole crown lavishly with buttons, creating a real conversation piece, or, if you feel less adventurous, you could simply highlight the brim or band.

Choose the buttons to complement the style of the hat, as well as the occasion. It is a good idea to tack the buttons in place on one thread to check the design first, before sewing each in their final position individually. Use a strong thread in a matching colour.

HAT TRICKS

The striking flower buttons decorating the band on the cream straw hat below add a lovely summery feel that would be perfect for a wedding or christening, or even a day at the races. Sportier felt hats, such as the one shown below left, can be trimmed with wood and horn buttons in natural colours, with the buttons positioned on one side of the band in place of a more traditional feather or flower decoration.

The brown felt "pot" hat on the right makes an ideal candidate for fun decoration – buttons can be sewn all round the rim, or even all over the crown, as shown here. The buttons on this hat have been sewn randomly, but you could sew them in patterns for a more "structured" look.

The crown of the "pot" hat above has been covered in a delightful assortment of quirky buttons collected over a period of time. They are of all shapes and sizes, and add a humorous touch that is both stylish and chic. On the other "pot" hat, on the opposite page, wood, leather and horn buttons have been used with the occasional golden highlight to decorate the brim and set off the dark brown base colour beautifully.

You can have a lot of fun with button decoration on hats, and could even decorate interchangeable bands to give the same hat a totally different look to suit both your mood and the occasion. Just let your imagination run wild and create your own totally original accessories.

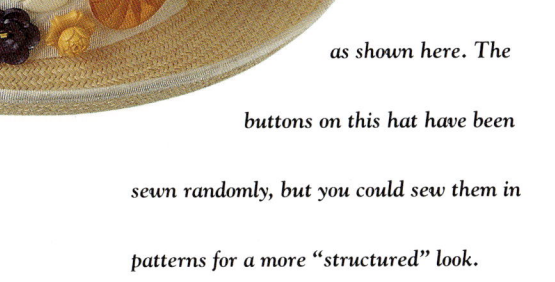

BUTTONED UP

Creative use of a jumbled collection of buttons can jazz up an uninteresting bag, giving it a designer look for little cost. Choosing a basic colour scheme adds a touch of flair.

A button trim can cleverly disguise a tired-looking bag and give it a fresh new look. You can also transform a cheap synthetic bargain quickly and easily, and no one will know that it hasn't cost the earth. Select buttons which will suit the shape and colour of the bag, and turn it into a covetable accessory. Diamanté buttons add a sparkle and are perfect for creating a glitzy evening look, while gold, silver and bronze buttons have an enriching effect, evoking the style of a bygone era. Be careful with polished finishes, as these can look too brassy and tend to

Pearly buttons turn this basic evening bag into an elegant accessory.

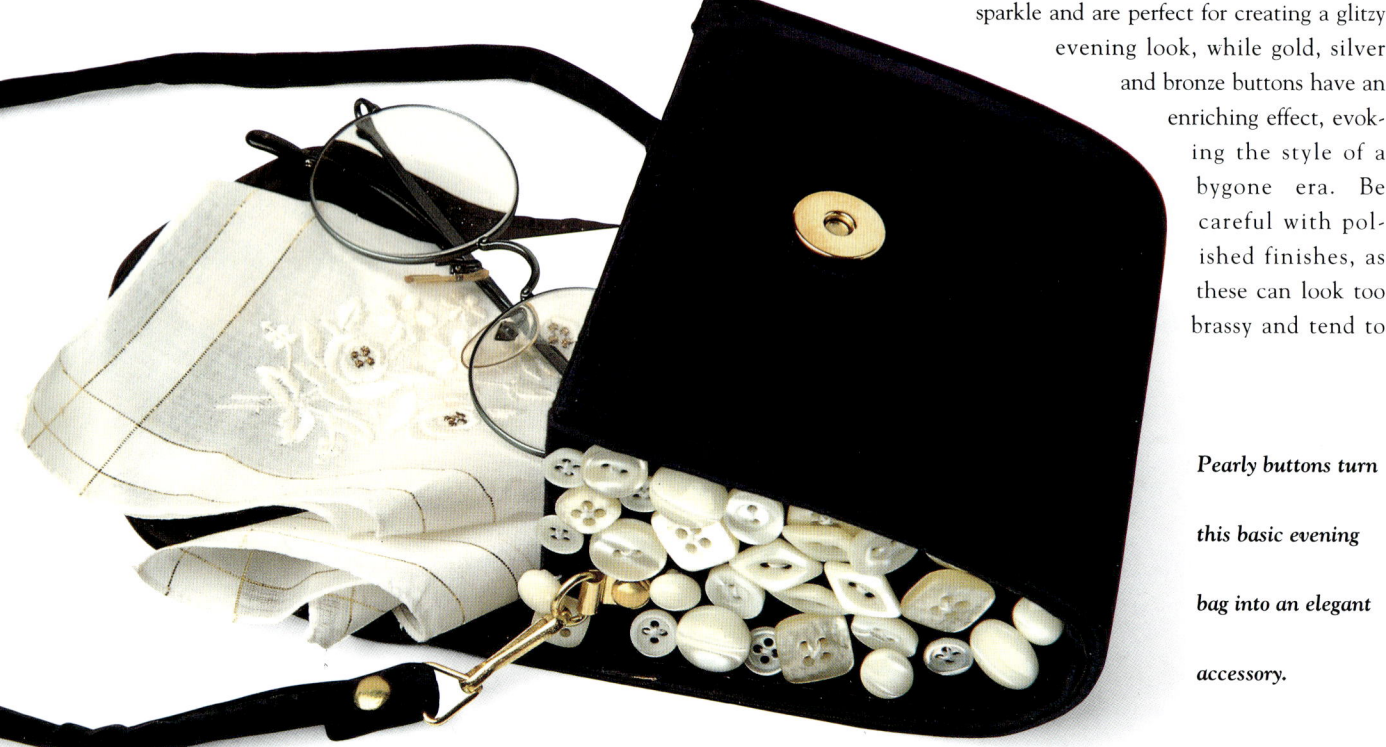

Buttoned Up

A red-and-gold colour theme was chosen here to set off the navy and create a bold but sophisticated look. Strong contrasts of this kind can be extremely effective. The gold in some of the buttons adds a rich touch of luxury, and also matches the strap fastenings to give the bag a "shop-bought" feel.

stand out unless they are surrounded by similar buttons. Grouped together, however, they really do look stunning, and bright young designers frequently use them for impact.

Your chosen design can be classy and understated, with the buttons sprinkled at random over the surface like gemstones, or bold and strong to inject a sense of humour. Strong primary colours can add a striking contrast to a plain background, as well as a touch of fun, brightening up the most ordinary and uninspiring of bags.

On the bags shown here, the buttons were stitched to the gussets on either side, overlapping each other to cover the area completely. Fabric and synthetic-leather bags are the easiest to decorate in this way, using basic sewing techniques. Be sure to use a fairly strong thread and to attach the buttons securely, as the bag may be subjected to a reasonable amount of wear and tear as it is carried around. It is best to stitch buttons in place on fine leather using a special leatherworker's needle with a fine point. With thick hides, you may need to use a bradawl (see page 8) to make holes prior to stitching the buttons in position.

TASTEFULLY TRIMMED

The ingenious use of buttons for trimming and decoration can refresh the most jaded or out-of-date clothes and accessories, giving them a stylish new lease of life.

Revamp an old leather belt with interesting button detail. Groups of buttons have been put together to create this simple design.

The fringed trim on this sweater was created by threading buttons together to make a long necklace. The buttons chosen were of different shapes and sizes, but were all made of wood, horn and leather to create a natural effect which complements the beige colour of the sweater.

You will need to work with two threads to hold the buttons in place. Start one thread by bringing it up through a hole in the first button, then put it down through the hole in the next button, and so on. The second thread runs parallel to the first but is worked the other way – that is, down through the first hole, up through the second hole, and so on. Leaving a small gap between each button, thread on as many as you require for the length, alternating the styles and shapes along the "necklace". Knot each end. Next, cut smaller lengths of string: you will need one piece for each gap between buttons. Fold each length in half and tie it over the two threads between each button as you would a gift tag – push the looped end under the threads, and then bring the other two ends up over the two threads and pull the ends through the loop. Knot to secure. Trim the fringe and knot wooden beads to the end of each "tassel" to finish.

To decorate a belt such as the

Tastefully Trimmed

The neckline of this plain V-neck sweater is enhanced with buttons made of wood, horn and leather. String emphasizes the "natural" effect, and also echoes the stitching on the leather buttons, setting off the rich brown colour scheme perfectly.

one shown on the left, the buttons can be glued in place, but, for a more durable finish, it is wise to stitch them in position. When decorating a thick leather belt, you may need to use a bradawl (see page 8) to start each hole. Work out the design first, and then sew each button in position using a strong thread and a special leather needle.

BUTTONS

Quite spectacular effects can be achieved by using lots of buttons with one underlying colour theme to accentuate an unusual accessory. The gold stripe on this classic tie was used as the base colour, and the tie was then decorated liberally with lots of gold buttons in all shapes and sizes to create an imaginative effect. The tie could be worn in the conventional way, or slipped through the belt loops on a pair of evening trousers or a skirt and tied loosely for casual flair.

Sew the buttons in place, using a fine invisible thread and

ALL TIED UP

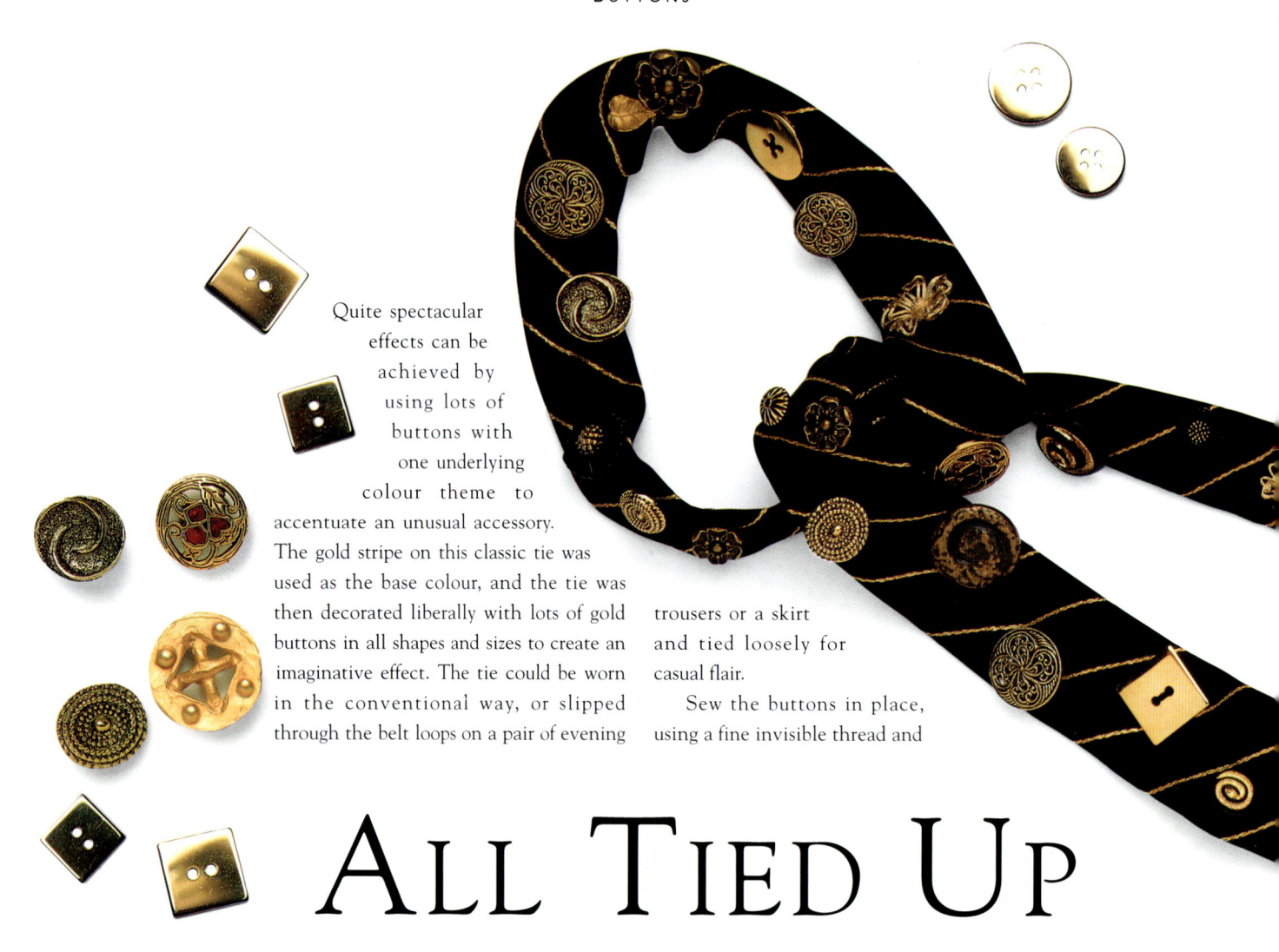

Take one basic tie, decorate it with a large assortment of gold buttons, and you have a brand new look that will add dash to your wardrobe and a touch of humour to any social occasion.

ALL TIED UP

This striped tie is lavishly decorated with varied gold buttons. A good starting point is to pick out a colour from the design on the tie, or from the background, and to use this as the basis for your button colour theme. taking tiny stitches.

The buttons can be sewn randomly all over the tie, as in the design shown here, or you could position them more uniformly, perhaps using just a few in one area to create a focal point. The intended purpose of the tie will obviously influence the placing of the buttons to some extent, so bear this in mind when you are planning your design. Choose rich metallic finishes and jewel-like colours for evenings, and bright primary colours or wooden buttons for day wear.

Use this idea to inspire you to create original accessories that you can be sure no one else will be wearing. Have fun playing around with different ideas and designs, and experimenting with colours and patterns, until you come up with something really effective. There are lots of other accessories which can be given the same treatment, such as scarves, stoles, hats, gloves, evening bags and even shoes, and there are more ideas for some of these throughout the book. You will soon realize that the possibilities are endless, and you will find yourself looking for different and unusual buttons everywhere you go.

ELEGANT EARRINGS

Beautiful buttons can be transformed into unique jewellery designs that will draw admiring comments. Use these ideas for earrings to inspire you to start looking through your button box.

Elegant Earrings

The lovely earrings shown here are just some of the many designs which can be created with a few buttons and a little imagination. They are all deceptively simple and quick to make.

Earrings are some of the easiest and most effective items to decorate with buttons, whether they are simple studs or ornate drops. Button jewellery is also an original way of using up odd buttons or displaying those too precious to use on clothing. Try combining antique or modern buttons to produce truly innovative pieces.

The simplest designs are easily made by gluing earring findings (either clips or posts and butterflies – see page 8) to the backs of a pair of attractive buttons, such as the crested blazer buttons with shank fastenings shown below. More interesting effects can be achieved by linking two buttons together with fine wire or glue. Small buttons with shanks can be wired to larger, hole-fastening buttons to create pretty stud earrings, or small beads can be strung and attached so that they cascade from the central holes.

Use simple silver-hoop earrings as a base, and decorate each of these with two crystal buttons to make a glamorous pair of earrings for evening wear. Create elegant drop earrings by linking the shanks of small gold buttons with jump rings to form loops, and then hang these from the shanks of larger buttons before adding the findings.

A glance through the selection of jewellery findings available will fire your imagination, and, once you get started, you will find yourself thinking up a wealth of designs. Have fun experimenting with and linking different shapes, sizes and colours of buttons in a variety of ways, and create your own unique collection of jewellery that will be the envy of your friends.

Buttons can be used to trim many different hair accessories, giving them a unique personal stamp or simply transforming them from practical daytime to more sophisticated evening wear.

HAIR DRESSING

Tortoiseshell-effect slides and combs look particularly attractive when combined with shell or pearl buttons. Padded black velvet or satin Alice bands look glamorous with sparkling diamanté and metallic buttons for evening wear. You could even continue the theme on other accessories to go with your outfit, such as a bag or shoes – refer to other projects in the book for ideas.

To make your own head-turning accessories, you need to experiment and plan your designs before securing the buttons. This is not always very easy on narrow, curved surfaces, but double-sided adhesive tape is perfect for holding the buttons in position temporarily while you work out the design.

When you come to sewing, you may find a curved needle useful to deal with any awkward angles. You can use thread to add some texture to the design by sewing on the buttons with fine ribbon or raffia, for example, or you can simply choose a matching colour or use an invisible thread.

For gluing, it is essential to use a glue that is suitable for the materials with which you are working, and to ensure that both surfaces are free from dust and grease. Wiping the surfaces with a lint-free cloth dipped in white spirit is one way of doing this. You may need to roughen the surfaces of some plastic materials slightly with emery paper before gluing – this will give a key and will ensure good contact.

Buttons make wonderful additions to all kinds of hair accessories, from combs to Alice bands. Choose toning or contrasting button colours to suit your outfit and your mood.

BUTTONS

Bold gold and black buttons on a velvet band make a stunning bracelet. This could be complemented by matching earrings or even a choker necklace.

BROOCH
& BRACELET

Button jewellery is really easy to make and produces truly original and individual pieces. No two designs will be the same, especially if you use antique buttons.

Brooch & Bracelet

It is possible to make attractive jewellery from just a small assortment of buttons by using a little imagination and ingenuity. The bracelet shown opposite was made with a mixture of antique and modern buttons to create a beautiful finished piece. To start the design, choose one or two buttons that you really like and create a colour scheme around them. Once you begin to see the possibilities, you will soon become addicted to searching out button shops and stalls in every town that you visit! Antique fairs, car-boot sales and jumble sales are other great sources for old buttons. Search through the clothes for interesting and unusual designs which could be snipped off and used for decorative purposes.

The buttons for this bracelet were sewn on to an elasticated velvet band to create a chunky, evening effect with a designer feel. The buttons were overlapped so that they totally covered the band for a really rich, ornate look.

The button brooch on this page was inspired by a wonderful seashell button which, alongside the mother-of-pearl and starfish buttons, created a seashore theme. Filmy ribbon conceals the cardboard base and gives a seaweed effect to tie in with the rest of the design. A scattering of small gold beads creates the impression of sand.

Let the buttons do the inspiring. Few people who become interested in buttons can resist building up a large collection, and you will find that, once you have spotted one or two buttons on a particular theme, you will start discovering them everywhere. Then you will find exactly the right button that could be worked into a design to set it off perfectly and create a really dazzling piece of jewellery.

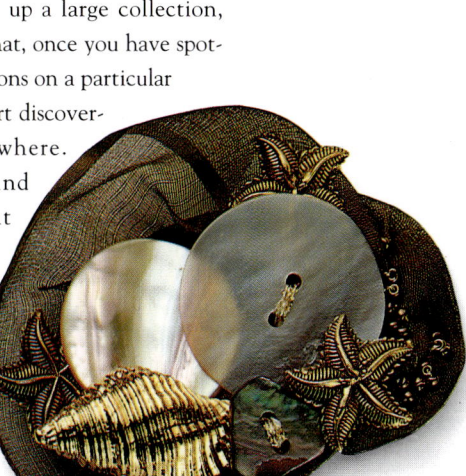

This delicate seashore brooch looks very intricate but is extremely easy to make. The mother-of-pearl button provides a perfect foil to the bright gold shell and starfish.

The buttons of this unusual neck cowl are enclosed in small "pockets" of machine-knitted nylon monofilament, although fine net would do just as well.

DIZZY DINOSAURS

design, or add some bright embroidery detail to continue the theme of the buttons, as on this jolly pair of gloves.

Making your own buttons is also great fun, and, with polymer-modelling clays such as Fimo, it couldn't be easier. See pages 10–11 for tips and techniques, and use the wide range of colours available to produce your own bold, attractive designs.

Button-making is also a good project in which to involve children, giving them the chance to create their own original works of art. Sewing on the buttons that they have made could even be their first sewing lesson if they are old enough, and if an adult keeps a watchful eye.

Depending on the design, buttons can be sewn on at random or used in groups to create motifs. A complete picture could be worked on the back of a sweatshirt using lots of different buttons to make a real talking point at a party.

Let your imagination and your children's ideas run wild, and really have fun customizing their wardrobes.

This pair of tartan braces is transformed with a few bright buttons. Blue and red have been used here to match the tartan, but any other bright colours would look equally effective.

As with boys' clothes, fun buttons in the shapes of well-loved characters or animals are a great way of dressing up a little girl's accessories and adding a personal touch.

ALL THINGS NICE

Novelty buttons are available in such a wide spectrum of colours and different shapes that you will find yourself spoiled for choice. Select buttons in co-ordinating shades to suit a particular outfit, or pick out vibrant, clashing colours to create a really eye-catching impact. Where most children are concerned, the brighter the buttons you use, the more they will love them!

Pink is by tradition most little girls' favourite colour, and this usually does seem to be the case. It was the colour chosen to decorate this simple headband, and it works well on the navy background. This particular little girl is mad about animals, so I selected cats and ducks as her main characters, and added hearts and a cheeky ladybird to complete the design. They were stitched securely on either side of the bow,

with allowances made for the "stretch" factor in wear. Be careful not to use too many buttons, as they may catch in the hair when the band is put on and taken off, and could also be uncomfortable when worn all day.

Lots of other little girls' accessories also make good candidates for button decoration, including belts, gloves, shoes and bags. Fabric bags are the easiest type to decorate, but a leather needle with its special point (see page 9) will also make short work of tough vinyl and hide.

Along with all the other projects for children in this book, it is essential that the decoration is fixed in place securely. Most novelty buttons are fairly small, so it is very important that little fingers cannot pull them off and put the buttons in a child's mouth.

BUTTONS

Dizzy Dinosaurs

All children love dinosaurs, and these bold-coloured buttons are just the thing to brighten up a little boy's braces and gloves and make them fun to wear.

Novelty buttons of popular characters are a great way of jazzing up a child's favourite outfit. Let children choose the buttons in the shapes of well-loved characters or animals, and then use them to give a lift and add a touch of humour to simple accessories such as gloves or hats, bags, hair bands, scarves and even drab school satchels.

These tartan braces and tomato-red gloves have been given a fun new look with bold tyrannosaurus and stegosaurus buttons in bright blue and red. You can simply use the buttons on their own, arranging them to make an attractive

Bright blue dinosaur buttons on children's gloves are enhanced by a basic embroidery design in white wool. The stitches used include couching, French knots and stem stitch.

SUNFLOWER SHIRT

Bright and shiny novelty buttons are a great way of personalizing children's clothes. Ordinary chain-store buys can be turned into desirable designer originals with very little time and effort.

With a little imagination, you can make an item really special by using the buttons to create a design that is a work of art. You can see on the shirt shown here that these sunny flower buttons look great with stylized stems and leaves embroidered to highlight the effect. Taking the buttons on to the pocket and collar and adding two ladybird buttons continues the theme.

Use the buttons to inspire added detail. Ducks and boats can have wavy lines embroidered underneath them to look like the ripples on a pond, for example, and simple stars can be made to look like shooting stars with a few small beads or stitches. There are all kinds of possibilities, and if you check out the novelty buttons at good haberdashers you are sure to find inspiration and come up with lots of your own unique and fun ideas.

Fruit-shaped buttons are easy to find, and can be used to create a fruit-bowl motif on a pocket, with different fruits used for the buttons and on the collar. Alphabet buttons are also widely available, and are fun when combined to spell out names, while numbers can be used to create a clock face on casual wear such as sweatshirts. Add a touch of humour to a school shirt or jacket with buttons in the shapes of pencils and pencil sharpeners.

NECK & NECK

There is a stunning variety of buttons available which look too good just to use in the traditional way, and which can be made into fabulously original jewellery.

Choose buttons to suit your design. Some of the wonderfully glamorous buttons on this necklace have glass-jewel stones which glisten under the light, and the burnished seashell buttons add an ornate, antique feel.

The buttons have shank fittings and were threaded on a length of jewellery wire with small gold beads interspersed to accentuate the rich effect.

The button decoration was worked in three sections – two identical side pieces and the centre drop – which were then oversewn to gold cord using invisible thread. To make each side section, take a piece of wire a little more than double the length required and thread on the buttons and beads. To prevent the buttons from dropping forward, fold the wire in half and thread this end back along the length, through the beads and looping over the button shanks. Use jewellery pliers (see page 8) to turn the end of the wire through the shank of the last button to finish it off neatly. Bind each shank tightly to the cord with invisible thread, hiding the thread among the beads and taking it through the cord every now and then to secure it. Leave a small gap at the centre front for the drop. Make this section in the same way, but turn the ends of the wire into a loop and then oversew this to the cord.

The beautiful neck cowl opposite is a wonderful way of using up odd buttons. Translucent fabrics, such as this nylon monofilament, can create a particularly delicate effect for evenings.

Rich gold cord provides the base for this splendid necklace, which would look stunning worn with a simple black dress.

BUTTONS

Colourful novelty buttons enhanced with embroidered stems make this plain white child's shirt really attractive. Buttons can be used in this way on almost any item of clothing.

The easiest way to give clothes a brighter look is to replace boring and uninspiring buttons with fun novelty versions. These are now available in all shapes and sizes and in fabulous jazzy colours that kids will love. Most are designed especially for children's clothing, so they should be both safe and washable, but check first if you are in any doubt.

ALL THINGS NICE

Pink and white animal buttons stand out beautifully on a navy headband. This type of elasticated band is widely available in shops and is also easy to make.

This shoulder bag is given a summery feel with butterflies and strawberries decorating the front flap and a couple of ladybirds adding a final touch. Matching buttons on summer sandals would also look pretty.

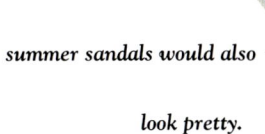

BUTTONS

Buttons can be used in lots of ways on cushions – create a colourful trim with tiny buttons, or use them as part of an overall design.

The clever addition of decorative buttons can give worn cushions a bright new look, and makes a refreshing change from the trims traditionally used. Experiment with different patterns, laying out the buttons on the empty cover to see the effect before stitching them in place.

Choose buttons to suit your décor. They do not necessarily have to be a matching set in an antique or contemporary style, but remember that,

ALL SQUARE

Flat buttons sewn through the cushion pad create an upholstered effect (right); a trim of pearl buttons on velvet, with a self-covered button in the middle, makes an elegant cushion (centre); and bright gold buttons of different shapes gleam on cream taffeta (far right).

All Square

unless the cushion is used purely for show, buttons can be quite uncomfortable to lean on. Bearing in mind this comfort factor, it is best to opt for fine, flat buttons which won't dig into the back.

An alternative is to give the cushion an upholstered look by stitching the buttons through the pad, as on the cushion shown on the left. This creates a more interesting effect, as well as making the cushion more comfortable to lean on. Position the buttons in place on the front of the cover, then stitch them in the normal way but take the thread through to the back of the inner pad, pulling it tightly to create a dent in the surface. You can also sew buttons in the same position on the other side of the cover at the same time.

The beautiful pearly finish of shell buttons decorating a cushion complements any room, especially a well-lit one where the lustre will catch the light. The small buttons used to trim the cushion in the middle create a really luxurious effect on the rich velvet background. Four triangles of fabric make up the top of this cushion, with a self-covered button (see page 10) sewn through the pad in the centre. On the right-hand cushion, pale taffeta provides the perfect foil to flat gold buttons. The large square buttons have been sewn through the pad, with the smaller buttons stitched to the surface only.

It is wise to choose washable or dry-cleanable buttons for cushions; otherwise you will have to remove them when the cover needs cleaning.

A pretty button and rings of coloured felt make an attractive variation of the upholstered cushion on the far left.

BUTTONS

Patchwork combines beautifully with buttons to give a "homely" feel. The buttons on this cover were sewn through all the layers to create a traditional quilted effect.

Patchwork, one of the oldest of home crafts, uses scraps of fabrics cut into shapes to form a pattern. These are then sewn together to form a whole piece of fabric with a mosaic effect, which can range from being subtle and understated to really bold and bright. Many different pattern shapes are used in traditional patchwork designs, but one of the simplest is based on the square, as used here.

This straightforward pattern is perfect for the beginner, provided that each square is cut to exactly the same measurement. You will find templates for the pattern shapes at most good craft shops, and using these

Quilted Treasure

The craft of patchwork is traditionally used to create pretty bedcovers, cushion covers and many other attractive items. This charming and simple-to-make quilt illustrates how effective the combination of patchwork and buttons can be.

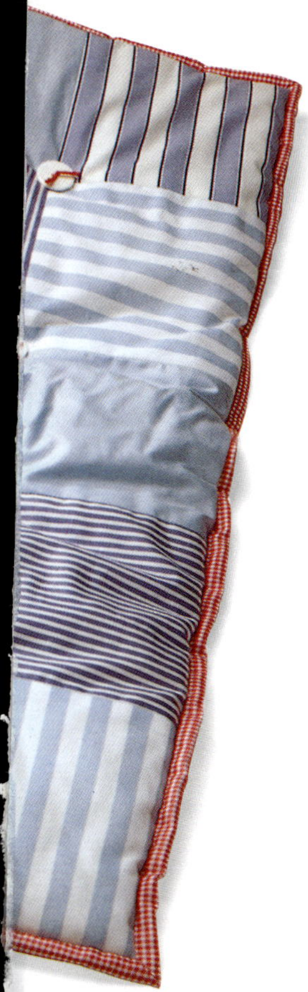

makes cutting the fabric into identical, regular shapes a much simpler task.

This delightful cover was made from a pretty patchwork of co-ordinating fabrics in bright fresh colours, ingeniously trimmed with buttons to create the quilted effect. Join the squares together to make a patchwork fabric that is the required size for your project. When you have finished this, join it to the backing fabric, with polyester wadding sandwiched between the two layers. Stitch all the layers together and sew bias binding around the edges to neaten them.

To complete the cover, sew buttons at the points at which the corners of the squares meet, sewing through the wadding and pulling the thread tight to create the quilted effect. As a decorative twist on the cover shown, stranded embroidery cotton of a contrasting colour was taken through each button and tied, leaving long, wispy ends. Make a small knot in each of the ends to prevent the cotton from fraying and working loose.

The finished cover is charming and would look good on any bed. It is, however, important to point out that it is not advisable to decorate babies' cot covers with button trims, just in case the buttons were pulled off and swallowed. The cover should be washed carefully by hand.

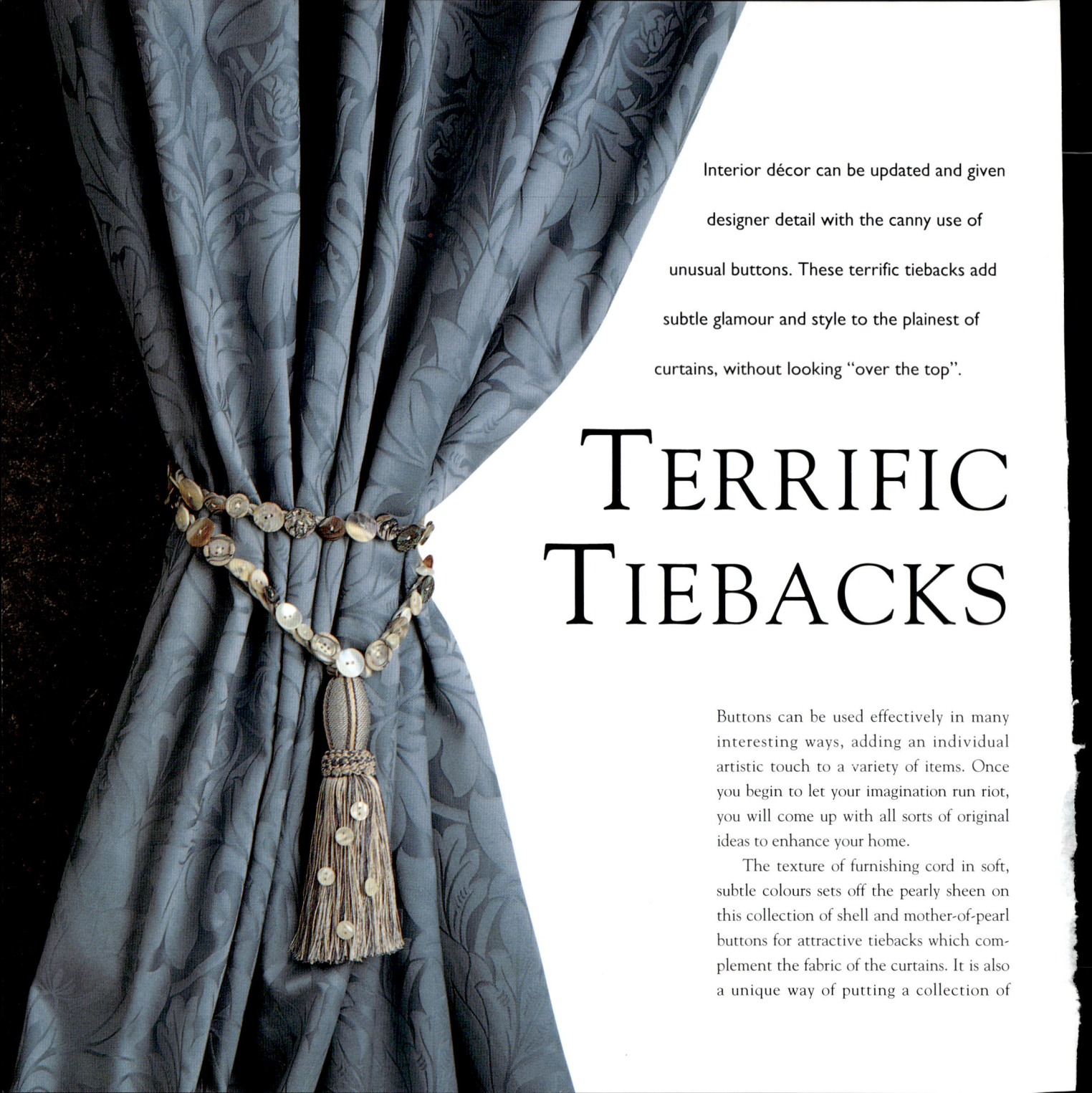

Interior décor can be updated and given designer detail with the canny use of unusual buttons. These terrific tiebacks add subtle glamour and style to the plainest of curtains, without looking "over the top".

Terrific Tiebacks

Buttons can be used effectively in many interesting ways, adding an individual artistic touch to a variety of items. Once you begin to let your imagination run riot, you will come up with all sorts of original ideas to enhance your home.

The texture of furnishing cord in soft, subtle colours sets off the pearly sheen on this collection of shell and mother-of-pearl buttons for attractive tiebacks which complement the fabric of the curtains. It is also a unique way of putting a collection of beautiful buttons permanently on show for all to admire, and is sure to be a real conversation starter.

The buttons can be sewn on to cover the cord completely, or to form a focal point of interest. You could also decorate fabric tiebacks in the same way to create an equally stylish effect. Choose buttons in colours to co-ordinate with the room for a harmonious look, but go for striking contrasts of colour if you wish to create a really dramatic impact.

The buttons on this cord tieback were sewn in position using a cream stranded embroidery cotton. Working with three strands together, take the thread through the centre of the cord and bring it out at the point at which the next button is to be secured. The finished cord can be topped off with an ornate tassel.

There are many other accessories for the home which can be given an interesting new look with some simple button decoration – just let your imagination run free and don't be frightened to be inventive.

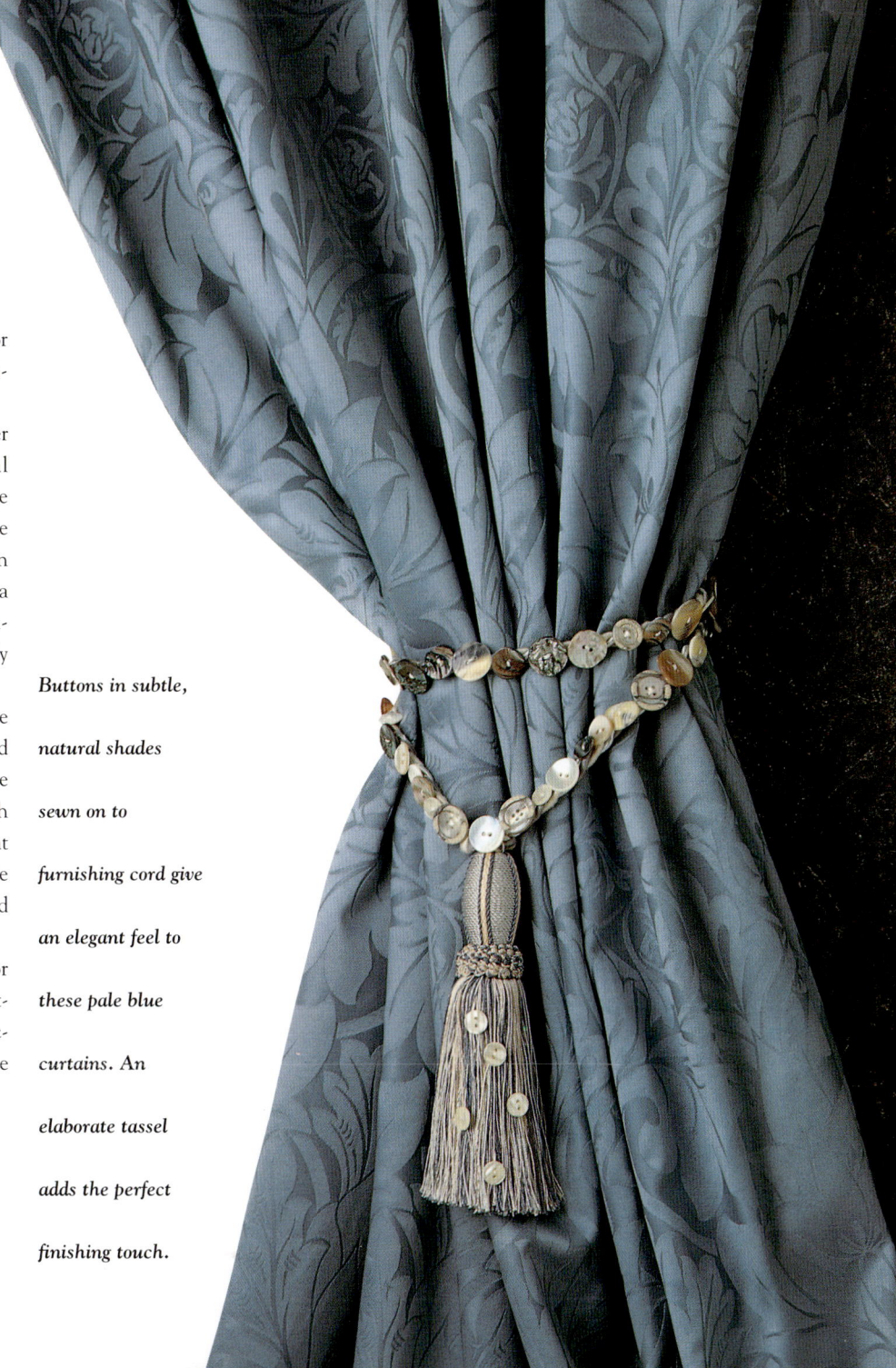

Buttons in subtle, natural shades sewn on to furnishing cord give an elegant feel to these pale blue curtains. An elaborate tassel adds the perfect finishing touch.

BUTTONS

HOT SPOTS

Bring a dash of style and a splash of colour to a child's room by cleverly trimming a variety of accessories with bold buttons in bright, sizzling hues.

Imaginative use of buttons in stunning colour combinations can achieve spectacular results. Once you start, you will find that even the most ordinary of objects can be given a jazzy new look using the simplest of decoration, as shown here. Toy boxes and other accessories can be revamped with buttons glued on as decoration, but be sure to use a tough epoxy adhesive so that inquisitive little fingers can't remove them.

The buttons on this lampshade and curtain look like a spattering of brightly coloured sweets or polka dots. The pattern on the curtain was worked out roughly first, and the position of the buttons marked with tailor's chalk. They were then sewn on in the traditional way to make them as secure and as child-proof as possible. If you are using buttons with shanks, choose a thread in a colour to match the fabric, but buttons with central holes can be sewn with brightly coloured contrasting thread to add extra zest to the finished appearance.

The same design was used to great effect on the lampshade. Here the buttons were made to look as if they were sewn in place, but they were in fact glued. Take a bright contrasting thread through the holes several times and knot it securely on the wrong side, and then use a strong, heat-resistant craft adhesive to glue the buttons firmly in position.

The beauty of these ideas is that, when the children get bored with the design, or grow out of it, the accessories can easily be replaced at little cost. Unpick the thread carefully and remove the buttons from the curtain and lampshade when you feel like a change, and re-use them for some of the other projects shown in this book!

The bright primary colours of these buttons really sing out against the rich cobalt-blue background of the curtain, and would make a perfect corner for a child's bedroom.

Pretty as a Picture

This romantic work of art was inspired by the Victorian era, and comprises a collection of old buttons, a couple of pieces of lace collected on my travels and a treasured card.

These lovely buttons lay unused and unappreciated at the bottom of a needlework box. I discovered the lace in Amsterdam in a shop selling bric-à-brac and thought that it was too precious to use on something frivolous, while the card, from a special friend, could not be discarded yet had no worthwhile use. Displayed together, they make the most enchanting picture of mementoes and treasures that would otherwise gather dust.

Having chosen your frame, you need to work out the size of your picture. Cut out a piece of craft interfacing to fit inside the frame exactly, and then a piece of fabric 5 cm (2 in) wider than this. Fold the fabric over the interfacing and stitch to secure it in place, making sure that the stitches don't show through on the right side. Arrange your treasures on the fabric, and stitch or glue them in place. Mark the position of the card with tailor's chalk, and then sew down the lace with invisible thread. The buttons for this picture were stitched on individually using embroidery silk, but, if you have a collection of antique buttons still on their original cards, they can look attractive displayed in groups and glued in place complete with the backing card. Use a clear-drying adhesive that is suitable for fabric both for the card keepsake and the buttons. Leave the picture until it is completely dry, press it carefully if necessary, and then place it in the picture frame and secure.

Treasure samplers such as this one make wonderful personalized gifts, especially as bridal or christening presents.

Birthday
VIOLETS·FOR·YOU
VIOLETS·FOR·ME
VIOLETS·FOR·ME
VIOLETS·FOR·ME
THE SHAKESPEARE
March 16th.
Tempest, Act II., Sc. 2.
March 17th.
All's Well that Ends Well, Act I., Sc. 1.
March 18th.
Tempest, Act I., Sc. 1.
BIRTHDAY BOOK

BUTTONS

CREATIVE CARDS

Interesting buttons can be used to make individual greetings cards with truly personal messages of good wishes, and in different styles to suit every possible occasion.

Card blanks are available in a variety of sizes and colours, and are perfect for making your own personalized greetings cards to send with love to your nearest and dearest. Decorate them with brightly coloured novelty buttons to welcome a new baby, to wish someone a happy birthday or just to say hello. You can draw extra detail on the front of the card blanks to complement the button design, and the borders look very

This small card made with white duck buttons positioned on a navy background is simple but very effective, and could be used for any festive occasion.

Bright, primary-coloured buttons resemble jazzy spotted wrapping-paper on the embroidered present, and would enhance any Christmas or birthday greeting.

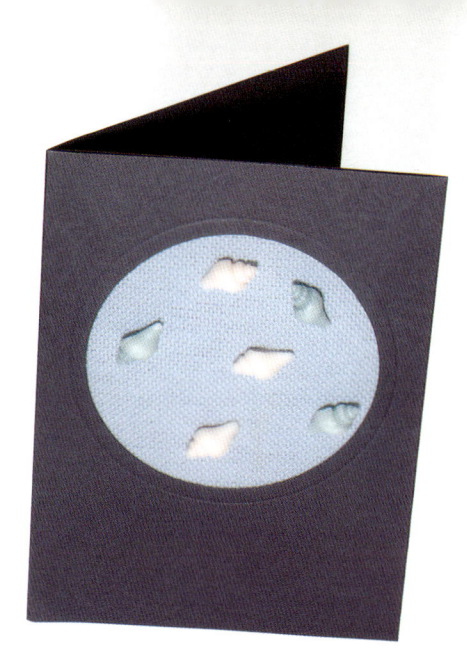

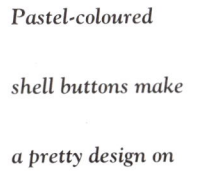

Creative Cards

Pastel-coloured shell buttons make a pretty design on this circular card blank. You can buy card blanks in many different shapes and sizes to suit all your design ideas.

fabrics can also be used to set off the pattern of the buttons. Work out the button design before stitching the embroidery design, marking the position of each button with tailor's chalk. Use stranded silk or cotton embroidery thread for words to suit the occasion, using cross stitch or a mix of stitches if preferred. There are many books and magazines available with charts of alphabets and borders which will inspire and help you. When the embroidery is complete, sew the buttons securely in place and mount the fabric inside a card blank, gluing it to secure.

effective when highlighted with gold or silver marker pens.

There is such a wonderful range of novelty buttons on the market that you will never be short of inspiration for creating cards suitable for any occasion. Flower buttons are available in a range of shapes and sizes, and these could be worked into small bouquets or placed as an arrangement in a vase. The only limit to what you can do is your imagination!

If you sew the buttons on to Aida (an embroidery cloth which comes in a variety of colours), you can work details and words in embroidery stitches, although other

Some delightful buttons in the shapes of prams inspired these new-baby cards, and the tiny toys completed the theme. These could also be used to make charming birthday cards for small children.

BUTTONS

It may be difficult to believe, but the delightful trinket boxes shown opposite started out life as containers for cheese similar to those below. A little creativity has transformed them and concealed their humble origins.

BOXING CLEVER

Traditional French-cheese boxes are often made from plywood and are far too good to throw away. Decorated with buttons and braid, they take on a new lease of life and make charming little boxes to give as gifts, or to keep on your own dressing-table or chest-of-drawers.

Any selection of buttons can be used. If you have only a few buttons, the design can be worked as a simple decorative motif or border, but the boxes do look especially attractive with their lids completely covered with an extravagant assortment of buttons.

Lightly sand the wood first, and then apply a coat of antique-pine varnish to deepen the colour. Glue braid around the side of the box to hide any writing before adding the button decoration.

Varnish will enrich and enhance the wood, but different effects can be

Empty cheese boxes in square or round shapes make ideal items for button decoration, and are just the right size to sit nicely on a dressing-table.

Boxing Clever

These pretty trinket boxes really look like expensive shop-bought items, but couldn't be easier to make.

achieved by painting the surfaces with acrylic paints. Cover with a primer such as white emulsion first, and then paint on the colour of your choice. Gold and silver are always attractive, and jet black can give the effect of Japanese lacquer. You could also try using decorative paint techniques such as marbling or faux verdigris and découpage around the side of an otherwise plain box.

Work out your design before gluing the buttons in place. Buttons with shank fittings will not sit easily on the top of the box while you do this, but some double-sided adhesive tape will keep them temporarily in place. Make sure that the surfaces are clean and free from dust to create a good contact (you may also need to roughen the surfaces slightly with an emery board to create a key). Use a clear-drying strong adhesive when totally covering a box, overlapping the buttons and letting them support each other. Leave the box for at least 36 hours to ensure that the buttons are set firmly.

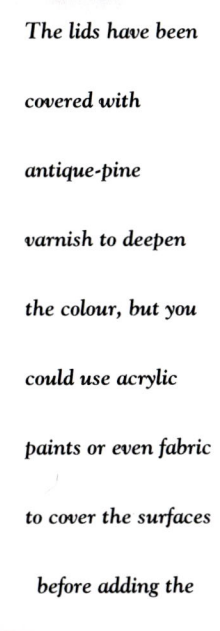

The lids have been covered with antique-pine varnish to deepen the colour, but you could use acrylic paints or even fabric to cover the surfaces before adding the buttons.

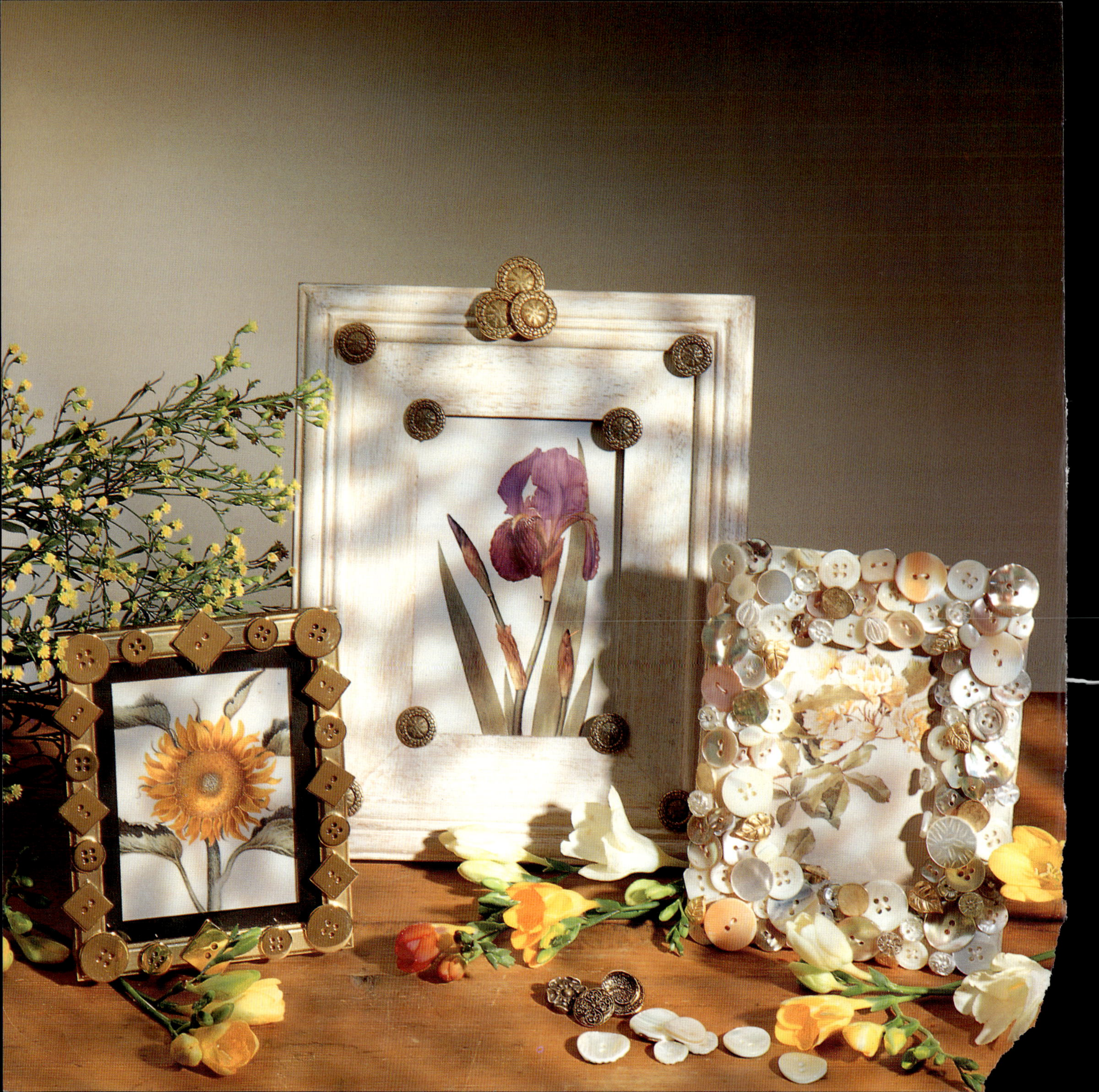

IT'S A FRAME-UP

Why not try mounting favourite photos in attractive frames of your own design? Creative button decoration can turn even the simplest, plainest frame into a work of art.

Picture frames look very effective either highlighted with or entirely covered by buttons. These cheap frames have been completely transformed using simple button decoration.

Polished, mirror-finish gold buttons in bold geometric shapes give a striking modern look to the cheap frame on the far left. The buttons were placed around the frame and juggled about until the final design was decided on, and then glued in place. Use a strong glue – a clear-drying one is best, as any excess won't spoil the design. If the glue spills out through the holes in the buttons, carefully remove it when dry. Both surfaces should be clean and free of dust and grease to ensure a good contact. Test one button first, letting it dry completely for 36 hours. If it comes away from the frame with little force, you may need to roughen the surface of the frame slightly with an emery board to create a key for the glue before sticking on the other buttons.

The old-gold buttons and limed-pine frame in the centre look as if they were made for each other. The buttons had shank fittings and were tricky to glue in place, so these were used to highlight the frame detail and positioned in the corners.

One side of the shank was glued to the side of the frame.

Matt-gold highlights added extra interest to the shell, mother-of-pearl and pastel buttons covering the right-hand fabric frame. The buttons were sewn using a curved needle threaded with stranded embroidery cotton. Using three strands, secure the thread under a button, where it won't be seen. Take the needle up through a hole, across the button and down through the other hole, bringing it up through the fabric at the position of the next button. Continue sewing on the buttons, overlapping them so that the frame is completely covered. When you reach the end of the thread, make a secure knot and then conceal this with a button.

BUTTON PEOPLE

Make these charming little people by simply stringing buttons together to form the bodies, arms and legs. Add a small ball to create the head, and top it with a button for a hat.

These cheerful button people will brighten up any corner of your home. Make five or six and turn them into a mobile for a child's room, or use them as novel decorative ornaments for the Christmas tree.

String your chosen buttons on to invisible nylon thread or matching cotton. Use different sized buttons – the smallest for the arms, medium-sized ones for the legs and the largest for the body. Buttons with shanks are ideal for the hands and feet, or you could attach bells to add a jolly jingle. The number of buttons required will obviously depend on the sizes used.

Cut two lengths of thread, each of approximately 46 cm (18 in). Fold one length in half, and push one end through a bell or the shank of a small button. Now take one end of the thread through one hole of a medium button and the other end of the same thread through the second hole. Thread on several more buttons of the same size to form a leg. Make up the other leg in the same way.

Next, take both ends of thread from one leg, and push them both through one hole in a large button to start the body. Take the two threads from the other leg through the second hole of the button. String on as many buttons as required to complete the body.

When the body is the correct size, separate the threads on one side and take just one of the pair through one hole in the smallest buttons to make an arm. When this is the right length, take the thread through the shank of a button to make the hand, and then take it back up through the holes on the other side. Repeat this for the other arm.

You can now add a button to make a neck if required, or simply take all four ends of thread through a hole pierced centrally in a pressed cotton ball to make the head. Knot the thread tightly, as close to the head as possible, to secure it. Trim the thread and add a blob of glue to fix the knot. Tie coloured or invisible thread to another final button to hang up the button person, and glue this to the head to make a hat.

Give your button people individual characters by selecting buttons to suit – create a clown with bright primary colours, for example, or a jolly sailor in classic navy and white.

ACKNOWLEDGMENTS

The author would like to thank the following people for their help and support while putting this book together. Firstly, Linda Collins and Terry Meinrath at Button Treasures who kindly supplied the majority of the wonderful buttons used to create the projects; Lesley Stanfield for her stylish designs; Lynn Galliver, Jackie Schou and Sandy Darby for their sewing skills, which were greatly appreciated; and last but not least my family, especially my mother and sister without whom the book would not have been completed.

Quarto would like to thank Button Treasures, 4 Charterhouse Buildings, Goswell Road, London EC1 for supplying the majority of the buttons used in this book.

Quarto would also like to thank the craftspeople who supplied projects for the book: Susie Freeman 38; Helen Milosavljevich 42; Lesley Stanfield 24-5, 28, 32-3, 48-9; Janet Slingsby 36-7, 40; Lesley Tonge 46. All other projects were made by Jo Moody.

Finally, Quarto would like to thank the models: Laura Bangert, Clara Chan, Giulia Hetherington, Laura Wickenden and Willoughby Werner.